ISBN 978-1-332-89182-5
PIBN 10433535

1 MONTH OF
FREE
READING

at

www.ForgottenBooks.com

By purchasing this book you are eligible for one month membership to ForgottenBooks.com, giving you unlimited access to our entire collection of over 700,000 titles via our web site and mobile apps.

To claim your free month visit:

www.forgottenbooks.com/free433535

English
Français
Deutsche
Italiano
Español
Português

www.forgottenbooks.com

Mythology Photography **Fiction**
Fishing Christianity **Art** Cooking
Essays Buddhism Freemasonry
Medicine **Biology** Music **Ancient
Egypt** Evolution Carpentry Physics
Dance Geology **Mathematics** Fitness
Shakespeare **Folklore** Yoga Marketing
Confidence Immortality Biographies
Poetry **Psychology** Witchcraft
Electronics Chemistry History **Law**
Accounting **Philosophy** Anthropology
Alchemy Drama Quantum Mechanics
Atheism Sexual Health **Ancient History**
Entrepreneurship Languages Sport
Paleontology Needlework Islam
Metaphysics Investment Archaeology
Parenting Statistics Criminology
Motivational

TO

HIS ROYAL HIGHNESS

PRINCE ALBERT,

AS THE PATRON OF SCIENCE

AND THE

PROMOTER OF WHATEVER TENDS TO THE KNOWLEDGE AND

INTERESTS OF HUMANITY

THIS

LITTLE SKETCH OF THE AZTECS' HISTORY

IS, WITH SENTIMENTS OF

PROFOUND RESPECT AND EXTREME GRATITUDE,

MOST HUMBLY DEDICATED.

PREFACE.

On Monday, July 4th, 1853, the AZTEC LILLIPUTIANS had the honor to be presented to Her Most Gracious Majesty. Having previously visited the families of Sir James Clarke, Sir Benjaman Brodie, Doctors Latham, Guthrie, Hodgkin, and been seen by Professors Owen, Grant, and Faraday, and the heads of the faculty generally, who considered them a curiosity so unique and extraordinary, as to warrant their commending them to the notice of royalty. At the palace, Her Majesty, their Royal Highnesses Prince Albert, the Prince of Wales, the Princess Royal, and the Princess Alice, viewed them with acknowledged gratification, and the pleasure they expressed was perfectly in accordance with the commendations bestowed on the Lilliputians by their Serene Highnesses the Prince and Princess of Prussia, Prince Holenlohe Langenbourg, the Duke and Duchess of Saxe Coburgh, and the other members of the Royal Party, present at the interview. Indeed, the excitement they occasioned at the Palace was far greater than that which their Guardians had expected, and the perfect satisfaction which Her Majesty and their Royal Highnesses were pleased to intimate will ever be one of the most gratifying reminiscences to those who have brought the Aztecs to England.

In the following pages the history of their discovery and that of the hitherto unknown city of Iximaya, whence they have been brought, will be found detailed with accuracy, translated in great part from the Spanish manuscript of Senor Velasquez, through whom they were originally obtained. For more extensive and interesting information concerning the unexplored regions to which they are related, we beg to refer the reader to Stephens's "Incidents of travel in Central America" Catherwood's magnificent work or Squiere's "Yuca·

LONDON, MORNING ADVERTISER, JULY 25th,

A throng of distinguised and fashionable visitors have honored these extraordinary and incomprehensible little problems of humanity with visits during the week. Their Majesties the King and Queen of Hanover, and the Crown Prince and Princess, and the whole of the late royal family of France, including the ex-Queen, visited the Hanover-square rooms; also the Duchess of Sutherland, Duchess of Bedford, Lord William Lennox, Duke of Argyle, the Duchess of Orleans, Lord and Lady Blantyre, the Duke D'Aumale, the Duke de Chartres, and the Count de Paris, Her Imperial Highness the Grand Duchess of Leuchtenberg, H. R. H. the Duchess of Cambridge, Her Serene Highness the Hereditary Grand Duchess of Mecklenburgh Strelitz, the Princess Mary of Baden, the Duke of Devonshire and party, the Duchess of Hamilton and family, Countess of Essex and Lady Adela Capel, Earl and Countess of Wilton, Earl and Countess Bruce, Lord Brougham, Lord Ward, Lord Boston, Marchioness of Aylesbury, Viscountess Ebrington, Countess of Kildare, Marquis of Waterford and Viscountess Canning, Earl of Harrowby, Earl of Hardwicke, Marquis of Clanricarde, Earl of Rosse, Lord Monteagle, Earl and Countess Powis, Lady Ann Dashwood, Lady Gage, Lady Smart, Colonel Weymouth, General Dumas, the members of the Turkish and Prussian embassies, Miss Gladstone, Mr. Sidney Herbert, Lord Tankerville and by many other members of the aristocracy. The ex-Queen of the French, not only expressed the great interest she took in the Lilliputian wonders, but substantially testified her approbation in the form of a valuable present. Her example has been imitated by many other visitors, and so numerous have been the contributions of the ladies in the way of jewels, toys, and habiliments, that the question may well be asked,—who would not be an Aztec?

OUTLINE ILLUSTRATIONS

FROM THE

RUINS OF CENTRAL AMERICA

OF ITS

ANCIENT RACES.

The accompanying engravings, sketched from the ruins of Central America, bear both in features and in position of the head, a resemblance all will readily detect to the Aztec children, found in the same country, and now being exhibited ; and who according to succeeding pages, belong to an ancient sacerdotal caste.

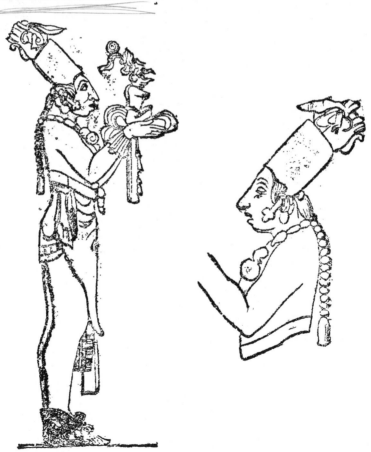

vi

The following, from Stephen's "Central America," may be regarded more immediately as the types of the existing members of that priestly caste, to which these children are assumed to pertain.

The characteristic resemblance of the faces sketched in the works of Central American travellers, to those of the people inhabiting the unknown regions of that country, is positively asserted by the Spanish author of the pamphlet. In an appendix to the original, he directs especial attention to the following figures.

THE MALE FIGURES.

In connexion with this, the author asserted that the Iximayans claim descent from an ancient Assyrian colony, a claim somewhat affirmed by the existing analogy, between the monuments of Nineveh, and those of Central America. Both are equally colossal and characteristic: but if our wonder is demanded, it is chiefly that in this remote country, far removed from European civilisation with no links that ever bound it to the old continent known to history. a people should unite in constructing such evidences of greatness, impressing these with the signs of lofty ideal superstitions, which associated all that was visible with a divine essence

vlll

THE FEMALE FIGURES.

It is perhaps, less singular, if the remnants of a sacerdotal caste should
have been preserved. The superstition that first enshrined them, would
serve to protect them. Some secret arcana would still be preserved in
which these sacred symbols of the deity might be beheld and reverenced.
Nor was it necessary, in order to the caste being thus regarded, that it
would possess any high mental qualifications.

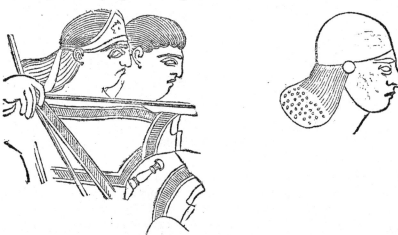

The two left hand Figures, sketched from Layard's Nineveh (see fore-
going pages) and the right hand profile from the same work are pronounc
ed by Velasquez to be equal'y characteristic of the female faces of that
region, making due allowance for the superb head dresses, of tropical
plumage, with which he describes it as being adorned, instead of the
male galea, or close cap retained in the engraving.

THE HISTORY

OF THE

AZTEC LILLIPUTIANS.

CENTRAL America and Yucatan, with their massive ruins of temples, palaces, and pyramids, have for centuries been regions of mystery. Travellers have not surveyed them with that accuracy which has been bestowed on other parts of the earth, and though we know something concerning them, it is a question whether that which we do not know surpasses that which is known. Mr. Stephens, in his great and remarkable work on Central America, speaks with enthusiasm of the conversations he had held with an intelligent and hospitable padre, or Catholic priest, of Santa Cruz del Quiche, formerly of the village of Chajul; and of the exciting information he had received from him, concerning immense and marvellous antiquities in the surrounding country, which, till then, had remained entirely unknown to the world. The padre told him of vast ruins, in a deserted and desolate region, but four leagues from Vera Paz, more extensive than Quiche itself; and of another ruined city, on the opposite side of the great traversing range of the Cordilleras, of which no account had been given. But the most stimulating story of all, was the existence of a *living city*, far on the other side of the great sierra, large and populous, occupied by Indians of the same character, and in precisely the same state as those of the country in general, before the discovery of the continent and the desolating conquests of its invaders.

The padre averred that, in his younger days, he had climbed to the topmost ridge of the sierra, a height of 10 or 12,000 feet, and from its naked summit, looking over an immense plain, extending to Yucatan and the Gulf of Mexico, had seen, with distinctness in the remote distance, " a large city, spread over a great space, with turrets white and glittering in the sun." His accounts of the prevalent Indian report was, that no white man had ever reached that city that the inhabitants, who spoke the Maya language, were aware that a race of white strangers had conquered the whole country around them, having murdered every white man that had since attempted to penetrate their territory. He added that they had no coin or other calculating medium ; no horses, mules, or other domestic animals, except fowls, "and kept the cocks under ground, to prevent their crowing being heard." The report of their slender resources for animal food, and of their perpetual apprehension of discovery, as indicated in this inadequate and childish expedient to prevent it, is, in most respects, contradicted in the account of the following adventurous expedition, which, if it may be relied on, obtained better information of the internal economy and condition of the people than could have been required by any Indians holding communication with places so very remote from the territory as Quiche or Chajul.

The effects of these extraordinary averments and recitals of the padre, upon the mind of Mr. Stephens, together with the deliberate conclusions which he finally drew from them, is best expressed in his own language.

"The interest awakened in us, was the most thrilling I ever experienced. One look at that city was worth ten years of an everyday life. If he (the padre) is right, a place is left where Indians and a city exist, as Cortez and Alvarado found them : there are living men who can solve the mystery that hangs over the ruined cities of America ; who can perhaps, go to Copan and read the inscriptions on its monuments. No subject more exciting and attractive presents itself to any mind, and the deep impression in my mind will never be effaced.

"Can it be true? Being now in my sober senses, I do verily believe there is much ground to suppose that what the padre told us is authentic. That the region referred to does not acknowledge the government of Guatemala, and has never been explored, and that no white man has ever pretended to have entered it, I am satisfied. From other sources we heard that a large *ruined* city was visible ; and we were told of another person who had climbed to the top of the sierra, but on account of the dense clouds rising upon it, he had not been able to see anything. At all events, the belief at the village of Chajul in general, and a curiosity is aroused that burns to be satisfied. We had a craving desire to reach the mysterious city. No man, if ever so willing to peril his life, could undertake the enterprise, with any hope of success, without hovering for one or two years on the borders of the country, studying the language and character of the adjoining Indians, and making acquaintance with some of the natives. Five hundred men could probably march directly to the city, and the invasion would be more justifiable than any made by Spaniards; but the government is too much occupied with its own wars, and the knowledge could not be procured except at the price of blood. Two young men of good constitution, and who could afford to spend five years, might succeed. If the object of search prove a phantom, in the wild scenes of a new and unexplored country, there are other objects of interest; but if real, besides the glorious excitement of such a novelty, they will have something to look back upon through life. As to the dangers, they are always magnified, and, in general, peril is discovered soon enough for escape. But, in all probability, if any discovery is made, it will be made by the padres. As for ourselves to attempt it alone, ignorant of the language, and with the mozos, who were a constant annoyance to us, was out of the question. The most we thought of was to climb to the top of the sierra, thence to look down upon the mysterious city; but we had difficulties enough in the road before us; it would add ten days to a journey already almost appalling in the prospective; for days the sierra might be covered with clouds; in attempting too much we might lose all. Palenque was our great point, and we determined not to be diverted from the course we had marked out."—Vol. II., p. 193—196.

"Two young men of good constitution, *might succeed*," said Stephens. It is now known that two intrepid young men agreed to undertake the perilous and romantic enterprise, incited probably by this identical passage in Mr. Stephens's popular work—the one, Mr. Huertis, of Baltimore, an American of Spanish parents, from Cuba, the possessor of an ample fortune, and who had travelled in Egypt, Persia, and Syria, with the view of inspecting ancient monuments; the other, Mr. Hammond, a civil engineer from Canada, who had been engaged for some years on surveys in the United States.

Amply equipped with every desirable appointment, including daguerreotype apparatus, mathematical instruments, and fifty repeating rifles, the latter as precautionary in the event of an armed expedition becoming necessary, these gentlemen sailed from New Orleans, arriving at Balize in the autumn of 1848. Here they procured horses and mules, and engaged a party of ten experienced Indians and Mestitzos. After pur-

suing a -route through a wild, broken, and heavily-wooded
region, for about 150 miles, on the Gulf of Amatique, they
struck off more to the south-west, for Copan, where they
arrived on the morning of Christmas-day, in time to partake
of the substantial enjoyments, as well as to observe the peculiar
religious ceremonies, of the great Catholic festival in that
secluded interior city.

Whilst loitering here to procure information and guides for
their future journey to Santa Cruz del Quiche, they became
acquainted with Senor Pedro Velasquez, of San Salvador,
who described himself as a man of family and education,
although a trader in indigo. His immediate destination, prior
to his return to the capital, happening to be the same city, he
kindly proffered to the two Americans the advantage derivable
from his superior knowledge of the country, as well as other
service in the form of negociations. He was accordingly
very gladly received as their friend and companion on the
way. It is from a copy of a manuscript journal of this
gentleman, that the translator has obtained what purports to
be the results of this exploring expedition, in the untimely fate
of Messrs· Huertis and Hammond, its unfortunate originators
and conductors, and the discovery of those extraordinary living
specimens of a race of beings, hitherto supposed either
fabulous or extinct, and which are at once its melancholy
trophies and its physiological attestors. For these statements
Senor Velasquez must be held responsible, as the matter only
admits of incidental corroboration.

In order, however, to avoid an anticipatory trespass upon
the natural sequence of the narrative, it may be proper to
state, that prior to his departure in their company from Copan,
Senor Velasquez had received from his fellow-travellers no
intimation whatever concerning the ulterior object of their
journey and had neither seen nor heard of those volumes
describing the stupendous vestiges of ancient empire, in his
native land, which had so strongly excited the emulous passion
of discovery in their minds.

Frequently called by his mercantile speculations to perform
long jouneys from San Salvador, on the Pacific side of the
Cordilleras, to Comyagua in the mid-interior, and thence to
Truxillo, Omoa, and Ysabal, on the Bay and Gulf of Honduras,
he had traversed a large portion of the country, and had often
been surprised with sudden views of mouldering temples,
pyramids, and cities of vast magnitude and marvellous mytho-

logy. As a man of unusual intelligence and scholastic acquirements, he had doubtless felt, as he states, a profound but hopeless curiosity concerning their origin and history. He had even seen and consecutively examined the numerous and ornate monuments of Copan ; but it was not until he had proceeded to the second stage of the journey from Copan to Quiche, that he was shown the engravings in the first volume of "Stephens's Central America," in which they are so faithfully depicted. He recognised many of them as old acquaintances, others as new ones, which had escaped his more cursory inspection ; in all he could trace curious details, which, on the spot, he regretted the want of time to examine. He, moreover, knew the surly Don Gregorio, by whom Mr. Stephens had been treated so inhospitably, and several other persons in the vicinity of the ruins, whom he had named, and was delighted with the *vraisemblance* of his descriptions. The senor confesses that these circumstances inspired him with unlimited confidence in that traveller's statements upon other subjects ; and when Mr. Huertis read to him the further account of the information given to Mr. Stephens by the jolly and merry, but intelligent old padre of Quiche, respecting other ruined cities beyond the Sierra Madre, and especially of the living city of independent Candones, or unchristianized Indians, supposed to have been seen from the lofty summit of that mountain range, and was told by Messrs Huertis and Hammond that the exploration of this city was the chief object of their perilous expedition, the senor adds, that his enthusiasm became enkindled to at least as high a fervour as theirs, and that, "with more precipitancy than prudence, in a man of his maturer years and important business pursuits, he resolved to unite in the enterprise, to aid the heroic young men with his experience in travel and knowledge of the wild Indians of the region referred to, and to see the end of the adventure, result as it may."

He was confirmed in this resolution by several concurring facts, of which his companions were now told for the first time. He intimately knew and had several times been the guest of the worthy Cura of Quiche, from whom Mr. Stephens received assurances of the existence of the ruined city of the ancient Aztecs, as well as the living city of the Candones, in the unsubjugated territory beyond the mountains. He alleges that he was the more induced to yield credence to the padre's confident report of the latter, because his account of the former had already been verified, and become a matter of fact and of record. During the preceding summer, Senor Velasquez, had himself joined a party of several foreigners and natives in exploring an ancient ruined city, of prodigious grandeur and extent, in the province of Vera Paz, but little more than 150 miles to the east of Guatemala (instead of nearly 200, as the padre had conjectured), which far surpassed in magnificence every other ruin, as yet discovered, either in Central America or Mexico. It lay overgrown with huge timber in the midst of a dense forest, far remote from any settlement, and near the crater of a long extinct volcano, on whose perpendicular walls, 300 or 400 feet high, were aboriginal paintings of war-like and idolatrous processions, dances, and other ceremonies, exhibiting, like the architectural sculpture on the temples, a high state of advancement in the arts. And as he knew from personal observation that the good padre had proved veracious and accurate on this matter, the senor would not uncharitably doubt his veracity on a subject in which he again professed to speak from the evidence of his own eyesight.

The party, thus reassured, and more exhilarated than ever with the prospect of success, proceeded on their journey. It cannot be doubted that Messrs. Huertis and Hammond considered Velasquez an invaluable accession to their party, as a guide on whom they could rely; and acquainted with the dialects of many of the Indian tribes through which they would have to pass, as well as familiar with the principal stages and villages on their route, knowing both the places and persons from whence the best information, if any, concerning the paramount object of the journey, could be obtained.

The senor's journal is fragmentary throughout, and relates to few incidents of travel between the capital of Vera Paz and Santa Cruz del Quiche. Under date of February 2nd, 1849, within this period of travel, he notes: "On the bank of a branch of the Salamo, attacked in the night by about thirty Indian robbers, several of whom had fire-arms. Senor Hammond, sitting within the light of the fire, was severely wounded through the left shoulder; they had followed us from the hacienda, six leagues, passed us to the north, and lay in ambush; killed four, wounded three; of the rest saw no more; poor Juan, shot through the body, died this morning; lost two mules."

The next memorandum is dated of the same month, 16th, when they had arrived at a place called San Jose, where Velasquez says: "Good Beef and fowls; Senor Huertis much better; Senor Hammond very low in intermittent fever; fresh mules and good ones." On the 5th of March, at the Indian village of Axitzel, is written: "Detained here five days; Hammond, strong and headstrong. Agree with Huertis that, to be safe, we must wait with patience the return of the good Cura." On April 3rd, the party arrived safely at Quiche, and were comfortably accommodated in a convent. The jovial padre, already often mentioned, who may be regarded as the unconscious suggestor of the expedition, had become helplessly, if not hopelessly, dropsical, and had evidently lost much of his wonted hilarity. He declared, however, that Senor Velasquez's description of the ruins explored the previous summer, recalling as it did his own profoundly impressed recollection of them, when he walked through their desolate avenues and deserted palaces; and corroborating as it did, in every particular, his own reiterated account of them, which he had often bestowed upon incredulous and unworthy ears, would "act like medicine to cure his malady and restore his spirits;" and if he could but live to see the description in print, so as to silence all gainsayers, he had no doubt it would completely re-establish him, and add many years to his life. He persisted in his story of the unknown city in the Candone wilderness as seen by himself, nearly forty years ago, from the summit of the sierra; and promised the travellers a letter to his friend, the Cura of Gueguetenango, requesting him to procure them a guide to the very spot from whence they could behold it for themselves.

This promise, in the course of a few days, the senor says he faithfully performed, describing from recollection, by the hand of an amanuensis to whom he dictated, not only the more striking but even minute and peculiar landmarks for the guidance of the guide. On the 10th of April, the party, fully recruited in health and energy, set out for Totonicapan; and thence we trace them by the journal through a succession of small places to Quezaltenango, where they remained but two days; and again through the places called Aguas Calientes and San Sebastiano, to Gueguetenango; this latter portion of their route being described as one of unprecedented toil, danger, and exhaustion, from its mountainous character, accidents to men and mules, terrific weather and loss of provisions. Arrived at the town last named, justly regarded by them as the critical stage of their destiny, they found the Cura, to whom

they presented the aforesaid letter of introduction. They
were somewhat discouraged on perceiving that the Cura indicated but little confidence in the accuracy of his old friend's
memory, asking them rather abruptly, if they thought him
really serious in his belief in his distant vision of an unknown
city from the sierra, because, for his own part, he had always
regarded the story as one of the padre's broadest jokes, and
especially since he had never heard of any other person possess-
ing equal visual powers. "The mountain was high, it was true,
but not much more than half as high as the hyperbolous
memory of his reverend friend had made it; and he much
feared that the padre, in the course of forty years, had so frequently repeated a picture of his early imagination as to have,
at length, cherished it as a reality." This was said in smooth
and elegant Spanish, but, says the senor, " with an air of dignified sarcasm upon our credulity, which was far from being
agreeable to men broken down and dispirited, by almost in-
credible toil, in pursuit of an object thus loftily pronounced a
ridiculous phantom of the brain." From this part of Senor
Velasquez's journal, we make the following quotation :—

"The Cura, nevertheless, on finding that his supercilious
scepticism had not proved so infectious as he expected, and
that we were rather vexed than vacillating, offered to procure
us guides in the course of a day or two, who were familiar
with many parts of the sierra, and who, for good pay, he
doubted not, would flatter our expectations to the utmost
extent we could desire. He advised us, however, in the same
style of caustic dissuasion, to carry a barometer and telescope,
if provided with those instruments, because the latter, especially, might be found useful in discovering the unknown city,
whilst the former would not only inform us of the height of
the mountain, but of the weather in prospect as most favourable
to a distant view. Senor Huertis replied that such precautions
would be adopted, further engaging to furnish him, on our
return to Gueguetenango, with the exact latitude and longitude of the spot from which the discovery might be made.
He laughed very heartily, and rejoining that he thought this
operation would be much easier than to furnish the same
interesting particulars concerning the location of the spots at
which the discovery might fail to be made : and saying this,
he robed himself for mass, which we all, rather sullenly,
attended.

" Next morning, two good-looking Meztitzos, brothers,

waited on us with a strong letter of recommendation from the Cura, as guides to that region of the sierra which the padre's letter had so particularly described, and which description the Cura added, he had taken much pains to make them understand. On being questioned concerning it, they startled and somewhat disconcerted us by calm assurances, in very fair Spanish, that they were not only familiar with all the land-marks, great and small, which the Cura had read to them but had several times seen the very city of which we were in search, although none but full-blooded Indians had ever ven-tured on a journey to it. This was rather too much, even for us, sanguine and confiding as we were. We shared a common suspicion that the Cura had changed his tactics, and resolved to play a practical joke upon our credulity—to send us on a fool's errand, and laugh at us for our pains. That he had been tampering with the two guides for this purpose, struck us forcibly; for while he professed never to have known any man who had seen the distant city, he recommended these Meztitzos, as brothers, whom he had known from their boyhood, they declared they had beheld it from the sierra on various occa-sions. Nevertheless, Senor Huertis believed that the young men spoke the truth, while the Cura, probably did not; and hoping to catch him in his own snare, if such had been laid, asked the guides their terms, which, though high, he agreed to without cavil. They said it would take us eight days to reach the part of the sierra described in the letter, and that we might have to wait on the summit several days more, before the weather would afford a clear view. They would be ready in two days; they had just returned across the mountains from San Antonia de Guista, and needed rest and repairs. There was a frankness and simplicity about these fine fellows which would bear the severest scrutiny, and we could only admit the bare possibility of our being mistaken.

"It took three days, however, to procure a full supply of the proper kind of provisions for a fortnight's abode in the sky, and on the fourth (May 5th), we paid our formal respects to the Cura, and started for the ascent—he not forgetting to remind us of the promise to report to him the precise geogra-phical locality of our discovery."

Four days thereafter, the writer says: "Our altitude, by barometer, this morning, is over 6000 feet above the valley which we crossed three days ago; the view of it and its sur-rounding mountains, sublime with chasms, yet grotesque in outline, and all heavily gilded with the setting sun, is one of the most oppressively gorgeous I ever beheld. The guides inform us that we have but 3000 feet more to ascend, and point to the gigantic pinnacle before us, at the apparant distance of seven or eight leagues; but that, before we can reach it, we have to descend and ascend an immense barranca (ravine), nearly a thousand feet deep from our present level, and of so difficult a passage, that it will cost us several days. The side of the mountain towards the north-west is perfectly flat and perpendicular for more than half its entire height, as if the prodigious section had been riven down by the sword of San Miguel, and hurled with his foot among the struggling multitude of summits below. So far the old padre is accurate in every particular." In a note appended to this extract, the writer adds: " The average breadth of the plain on this ridge of the sierra, (that is, the ridge on which they were then encamped for the night), is nearly half a mile, and exhibits before us a fine rolling track as far as we can see. Neither birds, beasts, nor insects—I would there were no such barranca !" He says, on May 13th: " On the brink of the abyss—the heaviest crags we can hurl down, return no sound from the bottom.

From entry of May 15th, we further quote :—"Recovered the body of Sebastiano and the load of his mule ; his brother is building a cross for his grave, and will not leave it until famished with thirst and hunger. All too exhausted to think of leaving this our first encampment since we descended. Present elevation but little above that of the opposite ridge, which we left on the 11th; still, at least, 3000 feet to climb." On the 19th, four o'clock, P.M., he records: "Myself, Senor Hammond, and Antonio, on the highest summit, an inclined plain of bare rock, of about fifteen acres. The padre again right. Senor Huertis and others just discernible, but bravely coming on. Elevation, 9,500 feet. Completely in the clouds and all the country below invisible. Senor Hammond already bleeding at the nose, and no cigar to stop it." At ten o'clock, the same night, he writes ; "All comfortably asleep but myself and Senor Hammond, who is going to take the latitude." Then follows : "He finds the latitude 15 degrees 48 minutes *no.th.*" Opposite this, in the margin, is written : " The mean result of three observations of different stars. Intend to take the longitude to-morrow." Next day, the 20th, he says : " A bright and most auspicious morning, and all but poor Antonio

IXIM YA DISCOVERED FROM THE SIERRA NEVADA

in fine health and feeling. The wind, by compass, N.E., and
rolling away a billowy ocean of mist, toward, I suppose, the
Bay of Honduras. Antonio says the Pacific will be visible
within an hour (present time not given); more and more of
the lower mountains becoming clear every moment. Fancy
we already see the Pacific, a faint yellow plain, almost as elevated as ourselves. Can see part of the State of Chiapas
pretty distinctly." At twelve o'clock, meridian, he remarks:
" Senor Hammond is taking the longitude, but finds a difference of several minutes between his excellent watch and
chronometer, and fears the latter has been shaken. Both the
watch and its owner, however, have been a great deal more
shaken, for the chronometer has been all the time in the midst
of a thick blanket, and has had no falls. Senor Huertis, with
the glass, sees whole lines and groups of pyramids, in Chiapas.
At one o'clock, P.M., he records: '· Senor Hammond, reports
the longitude, 92 degrees 15 minutes *west*. Brave Huertis is
in ecstacy with some discovery, but will not part with the
glass for a moment. No doubt it is the padre's city, for it is
precisely in the direction he indicated. Antonio says he can
see it with his naked eye, although less distinctly then here-
tofore. I can only see a white straight line, like a ledge of
limestone rock, on an elevated plain, at least twenty leagues
distant, in the midst of a vast amphitheatre of hills, to the
north-east of our position, toward the State of Yucatan, Still,
it is no doubt the place the padre saw, and it may be a great
city."

A memorandum at two o'clock, P.M.: " All doubt is at an
end. We have all seen it through the glass, as distinctly as
though it were but a few leagues off, and it is now clear and
bright to the unaided eye. It is unquestionably a richly
monumented city, of vast dimensions, within lofty parapeted
walls, three or four miles square, inclined inward in the
Egyptian style; and its interior domes and turrets have an
emphatically oriental aspect. I should judge it to be not
more then twenty-five leagues from Ocosingo, to the eastward,
and nearly in the same latitude; and this would probably be
the best point from which to reach it, travelling due east,
although the course of the river Legartos seems to lead directly
to it. That it is still an inhabited place, we infer from the
domes of its temples, or churches. Christian churches they
cannot be, for such a city would have an Archbishop, and be
well known to the civilized world. It must be a pagan strong-

hold that escaped the conquest by its remote position, and the
general retreat, retirement, and centralizing seclusion of its
surrounding population. It may now be opened to the light
of the true faith."

They commenced their descent the same day, and rested at
night on the place of their previous encampment, a narrow
shelf of the sierra. Here, on the brink of a terrible ravine,
which they had again to encounter, they consulted upon a
plan for their future operations, and it was finally agreed that
Messrs. Huertis and Hammond, with Antonio, and such of
the Indian muleteers as could be induced to proceed with the
expedition, should follow the bottom of the ravine, in its north-
east course, in which, according to Antonio the river Legartos
took its principle supply of water, and remain at a large
village, adjacent to its banks, which they had seen, about five
leagues distant; while Senor Velasquez was to trace their
late route, by way of Gueguetenango, to Gueguetenango, where
all the surplus arms and ammunition had been deposited, and
recruit a strong party of Indians, to serve as a guard, in the
event of an attack from the people of the unexplored region,
whither they were resolutely bound. In the meantime,
Antonio was, to return home to Gueguetenango, await the
return of Velasquez, with his armed party, from Quezaltenango, and conduct them over the mountains to the village
on the plains where Messrs. Huertis and Hammond were to
remain until they should arrive. It appears that Senor
Velasquz was abundantly supplied with solid funds for the
recruiting service, and that Mr. Huertis also furnished Antonio
with a liberal sum, in addition to his stipulated pay, where-
with to procure masses for the repose of his unfortunate
brother.

On July 8th, the party had arrived with "nearly all the
men he had engaged," at an Indian village called Agua-
masiuta, where Velasquez's anxious companions where over-
joyed to receive him, and where "they had obtained inesti-
mable information regarding the proper arrangement of the
final purpose." For a few days the devious course of the
Legartos was pursued. The remaining narrative of the expedition was written by Senor Velasquez from memory, after
his return from San Salvador, while all the exciting events
and scenes which it describes were vividly sustained by the
feeling which they originally inspired. As this excessively
interesting document will be translated for the public press as

soon as the necessary consent of its present proprietor can be obtained, the writer of this pamphlet less regrets the very limited use of it to which he is now restricted—which is but little more than that of making a mere abridgment and connexion of such incidents as may serve to explain the origin and possession of those specimens of humanity, the Aztec Lilliputians now exhibited to the public. The following is the introductory paragraph :—

"Our latitude and longitude were now about 17 deg. north, and 90 deg. 45 min. west; so that the grand amphitheatre of hills, forming three-fourths of an oval outline of jagged summits, a few leagues before us, most probably inclosed the mysterious object of our anxious and uncertain labours. The small groups of Indians through which we had passed, in the course of the day, had evidently been startled, by sheer astonishment, into a sort of passive and involuntary hospitality but maintained a stark apprehensive reserve in most of their answers to our questions. They spoke a peculiar dialect of the Maya, which I had never heard before, and had great difficulty in comprehending, although several of the Maya Indians of our party understood it familiarly and spoke fluently. From them we learned that they had never seen, men of our race before, but that a man of the same race as Senor Hammond, who was of a bright florid complexion, with light hair and red whiskers, had been sacrificed and eaten by the Macbenachs, or priests of Iximaya, the great city among the hills, about thirty moons ago. Our interpreters stated that the word "Iximaya" meant the "Great Centre," and that "Macbenach" meant the "Great Son of the Sun." I at once resolved to make the most of my time in learning as much as possible of this dialect from these men, because they said it was the tongue spoken by the people of Iximaya and the surrounding region. It appeared to me to be merely a provincial corruption or local peculiarism of the great body of the Maya language, with which I was already acquainted; and, in the course of the next day's conversation, I found that I could acquire it with much facility."

To this circumstance, the writer, if the account be authentic, is probably indebted for his life. Another day's journey, and the determined explorers had come within the circuit of the alpine district in which Iximaya is situated. They found it reposing, in massive grandeur, in the centre of a perfectly level plain, about five leagues in diameter, at a distance of scarcely two from the spot they had reached. At the base of all the mountains, rising upon their sides, and extending nearly a mile inward upon the plain, was a dark green forest of heavy trees and florid shubbery ; whilst the even valley itself exhibited large tracts of uncultivated fields, fenced in with palisades, and regular, even to monotony, both in size and form. "Large herds of deer, cattle, and horses, were seen in the openings of the forest, and dispersed over the plain, which was also studded with low flat-roofed dwellings of stone, in small detached clusters, or hamlets. Rich patches of forest, of irregular forms, bordered with gigantic aloes, diversified the landscape in effective contrast with bright lakes of water which glowed among them."

While the whole party, with their cavalcade of mules and baggage, were gazing upon the scene, two horsemen, in bright blue and yellow tunics, and wearing turbans decorated with three large plumes of the squezal, dashed by them from the forest, at the distance of about two hundred yards, on steeds of the highest Spanish mould, followed by a long retinue of athletic Indians equally well mounted, clothed in brilliant red tunics, with coronals of gay feathers, closely arranged within a band of blue cloth. Each horseman carried a long spear, pointed with polished metal ; and each held, in a leash, a brace of powerful bloodhounds, which were also of the purest Spanish breed. The two leaders of this troop, who were Indians of commanding air and stature, suddenly wheeled their horses and glared upon the large party of intruders with fixed amazement. Their followers evinced equal surprise, but forgot not to draw up in good military array, while the bloodhounds leapt and raged in their thongs.

"While the leaders," says Senor Velasquez, "seemed to be intently scrutinizing every individual of our company, as if silently debating the policy of an immediate attack, one of the Maya Indians, of whom I had been learning the dialect, stepped forward and informed us that they were a detachment of rural guards, a very numerous military force, which had been appointed from time immemorial, or, at least from the time of the Spanish invasion, to hunt down and capture all strangers of a foreign race that should be found within a circle of twelve leagues of the city ; and he repeated the statement m ade to us from the beginning, that no white man had hitherto eluded their vigilance, or left their city alive. He said there was a tradition that many of the pioneers of Alvarado's army had been cut off in this manner, and never heard of more, while their skulls and weapons are to this day suspended round the alter of the pagan gods. He, added, finally, that if we wished to escape the same fate, now was our only chance; that as we numbered thirty-five, all armed with repeating rifles, we could easily destroy the present detachment, which amounted to, but fifty, and secure our retreat before another could come up; but that, in order to do this, it was necessary first to shoot the dogs, which all our Indians regarded with the utmost dread and horror.

"I instantly felt the force of this advice, in which also I was sustained by Senor Hammond; but Senor Huertis, whom, as the leader of the expedition, we were all bound and solemnly pledged to obey: utterly rejected the proposition. He had come so far to see the city, and see it he would, whether taken thither as a captive or not, and whether he ever returned from it or not; that this was the contract originally proposed, and to which I had assented; that the fine troop before us was evidently not a gang of savages, but a body of civilized men and good soldiers; and as to the dogs, they were noble animals of the highest blood he ever saw. If, however, I and his friend Hammond, who seemed afraid of being eaten, in preference to the fine beef and venison which he had seen in such profusion on the plain, really felt alarmed at the bugbear legends of our vagabond Indians, before any demonstration of hostility had been made, we were welcome to take two-thirds of the men and mules and make our retreat as best we could, while he would advance with Antonio and the remainder of the party, to the gates of the city, and demand a peaceable admission. I could not but admire the romantic intrepidity of this resolve, though I doubted its discretion; and assured him I was ready to follow his example and share his fate.

"While this conversation was passing among us, the Indian commanders held a conference apparently as grave and important. But just as Senor Huertis and myself had agreed to advance towards them for a parley, they separated without deigning a reply to our salutation—the elder and more highly decorated galloped off towards the city with a small escort, while the other briskly crossed our front at the head of his squadron, and entered the forest nearer the enterance of the valley. This opening in the hills was scarcely a quarter of a mile wide, and but a few minutes elapsed before we saw a single horseman cross it toward the wood on the opposite side.

Presently another troop of horse, of the same uniform appearance as the first, were seen passing a glade of the wood which
the single horseman had penetrated, and it thus became evident
that a manœuvre had already been effected to cut off our
retreat. The mountains surrounding the whole area of the
plain were absolutely perpendicular for three-fourths of their
altitude, which was no where less than a thousand feet ; and
from many parts of their wildly piled outline, huge crags pro-
jected in monstrous mammoth forms, as if to plunge to the
billows of forest beneath. At no point of this vast impassable
boundary was there a chasm or declivity disernable by which
we could make our exit, except the one thus formidably
intercepted.

"To retire into the forest and water our mules at a copious
stream which rushed forth from its recesses, and recruit our
own exhausted strength with food and rest, was our first
necessary resourse. Iu tracing the rocky course of the current
for a convenient watering-place, Antonio discovered that it
issued from a cavern, which through a mere fissure exteriorly,
was, within, a cathedral dimensions and solemnity: we all
entered it and drank eagerly from a foaming basin, which it
immediately presented to our fevered lips. Our first sensations
were those of freedom and independence, and of that perfect
security which is the basis of both. It was long since we had
slept under a roof of any kind, while here a few men could
defend our repose against an assault from thousands ; but it
was horribly evident to my mind, that a few watchful assailants
would suffice to reduce us to starvation, or destroy us in detail.
Our security was that of a prison, and our freedom was limited
to its walls. Happily, however, for the present hour, this reflection seemed to trouble no one. Objects of wonder and
veneration grew numerous to our gaze. Gigantic statues of
ancient warriers, with round shields, arched helmets, and
square breast-plates, curiously latticed and adorned, stood
sculptured in high relief, with grave faces and massive limbs,
and in the regular order of columns round the walls of this
grand mausoleum. Many of them stood arrayed in the crimson
of the setting sun, which then flamed through the tall fissure
into the cavern ; and the deep gloom into which long rows of
others utterly retired from our view, presented a scene at once
of mingled mystery and splendour. It was evidently a place
of great and recent resort, both for men and horses, for
plentiful supplies of fresh fodder for the latter were heaped in

stone recesses. while the ashes of numerous fires, mingled with discarded mocassins and broken pipes and pottery, attested a domiciliarly occupation by the former. Farther into the interior were found seats and sleeping couches of fine cane work ; and in a spacious recess, near the entrance, a large collection of the bones, both of the ox and the deer, with hides also of both, but newly flayed and suspended on pegs by the horns. These last evidences of good living had more effect upon our hungry Indians than all the rest, and within an hour after dark, while we were seeking our first sleep, four fine deer were brought in by about a dozen of our party, whom we supposed to have been faithfully guarding our citadel. It is unnecessary to say that we gladly arose to the rich repast that ensued, for we had eaten nothing but our scanty allowance of tortillas for many days, and were in the lassitude of famine."

In the morning about the break of day, the infernal yells of a pack of bloodhounds suddenly rang through the cavern, and the party could scarcely seize their rifles before many of the dogs, who had driven in the affrighted Indians on guard were springing at their throats. Mr. Huertis, however, the American leader of the expedition, with that presence of mind which seems always to have distinguished him, told the men that rifles were useless in such a contest, and that the hounds must be dispatched with their long knives as fast as they came in, while the fire-arms were to be reserved for their masters. This canine butchery was accomplished with but little difficulty none of the party received any serious injury from their fangs; and the Indians were exhilarated with a victory which was chiefly a conquest of their fears. These unfortunate dogs, it appears, were the advanced van of a pack, or perhaps merely a few unleashed as scouts, to others held in reserve, for no more were seen or heard for some time. Meanwhile, Mr. Huertis seems to have struck out a brilliant scheme. He collected his whole party into that obscure branch of the cavern near its entrance which has been described as a depository of animal bones, and ordering them to sling their rifles at their backs, bade them stand ready with their knives. Almost instantly, they observed a party of ten dismounted natives, in scarlet tunics, and armed with spears, enter the cavern in single file ; and, it would seem, from seeing the dogs slain, and no enemy in sight they rushed out again, without venturing on farther search. In a few minutes, however they

returned with forty **or fifty men,** in the same uniform, headed
by the younger of the **two** personages whom they had seen in
command the previous evening. As soon as they were well
advanced into the cavern, and heard disturbing the tired
mules, Mr. Huertis and his party marched quietly out and
seized their horses, which were picketed close by, in charge
of two or three men, whom they disarmed. At a short distance, however, drawn up in good order, was another squadron
of horses, which Mr. Huertis determined instantly to charge.
Ordering his whole party to mount the noble animals they
had captured, and reserve their fire until he gave the word,
he, Velasquez, and Hammond, drew the short sabres they
had worn on their march, and led the attack. The uniformed
natives, however, did not wait the encounter, but scattered in
wonderment and consternation; doubtless under the impression that all their comrades had been slain. But the rapid
approach of a much larger force, which was found eventually,
to have consisted of two detachments of fifty each, being just
twice their number—speedily reassured them, and falling in
line with this powerful reinforcement, the whole hundred and
fifty charged upon our comparative handful of travellers,
at a rapid pace Heurtis promptly ordered his little party to
halt, and form in line, two deep, with presented arms; and
doubtless feeling that, notwithstanding the disparity of numbers, the enemy, armed only with spears and small side hatchets, held but a slender chance of victory over a party of
thirty-eight—most of them old campaigners in the sanguinary
expeditions of the terrible Carrera—armed with new " six-
shooting" rifles and long knives, generously commanded them
to keep aim upon the horses only, until further orders. In
the meantime, most of their plumed opponents, instead of
using their long spears as in lance practice, threw them through
the air from so great a distance that nearly all fell short of the
mark—an infallible indication both of timidity and inexperience
in action. The unfortunate Mr. Hammond, however, was
pierced through the right breast, and another of the party
was killed by being transfixed through the abdomen. At this
instant Huertis gave the word to fire; and, at the next, no
small number of the enemy were rolling upon the sod, amid
their plunging horses. A second rapid but well-delivered
volley, brought down as many more, when the rest, in attitudes
of frantic wonder and terror, unconsciously dropped their
weapons, and fled like affrighted fowls under the sudden swoop

of the kite. Their dispersion was so outrageously wild and complete, that no two of them could be seen together as they radiated over the plain. The men and horses seemed impelled alike by a preternatural panic; and neither Cortez in Mexico, nor Pizarro in Peru ever witnessed greater consternation at fire-arms among a people, who, for the first time, beheld their phenomena and effects—when mere hundreds of invaders easily subjugated millions of natives, chiefly by this appalling influence—than was manifested by these Iximayans on this occasion. Indeed, it appears that these primitive and isolated people holding no intercourse whatever with the rest of mankind, were as ignorant as their ancestors even of the existence of this kind of weapon; and although their modern hieroglyphical annals were found to contain vague allusions to the use of them in the conquest of the surrounding country, by means of a peculiar kind of thunder and lightning; and several old Spanish muskets and pistols were found in their scant collection of foreign curiosities, yet not even the most learned of their priests had retained the slightest notion of the uses for which they were designed.

While this summary conflict was enacted on the open lawn of the forest, the dismounted company in the cavern having completed their fruitless search for the fugitives, emerged from its portal with all the mules and baggage, just in time to see and hear the fiery explosions of the rifles and their effect upon the whole body of scarlet cavalry. The entire scene, including the mounted possession of their horses by uncouthly-attired strangers, previously invisible, must have appeared to these terror-stricken natives an achievement of supernatural beings. And when Mr. Huertis wheeled his obstreperously laughing party to recover his mules, he found most of the astounded men prostrate upon their faces, while others, more self-possessed, knelt upon the bended knee, and, with drooping heads, crossed their hands behind them to receive the bonds, of captives. Their gallant and gaily-accoutred young chieftain, however, though equally astonished and dismayed, merely surrendered his javelin as an officer would his sword, under the like circumstances, in civilized warfare. But, with admirable tact and forethought, Huertis declined to accept it, immediately returning it with the most profound and deferential cordiality of manner. He at the same time informed him, through Velasquez, that, though strangers, his party were not enemies but friendly visitors, who, after a long and painful journey, again to be pursued, desired the temporary hospitality of his countrymen in their magnificent city.

The young chief replied, with evident discomposure and concern, that his countrymen showed no hospitality to strangers; that the inhabitants of their city held intercourse only with the population of the surrounding valley, who were restricted alike by law and by patriotism from ever leaving its confines; he and his fellow soldiers alone being privileged to visit the neighbouring regions for the purpose of arresting intruders (*cowana*), and escorting certain kind of merchandize which they exchanged with a people of their own race in an adjoining district. He added, with much eloquence of manner, and as Velasquez believed, of language, which he but partially understood, that the independence and peace of his nation, who were a peaceful and happy people, depended upon these severe restrictions, which indeed had been the only means of its preservation.

He further added, says Velasquez, that some few strangers, it was true, had been taken to the city by its guards in the course of many generations, but that none of them had been allowed an opportunity of betraying its existance and locality to the cruel repacity of the foreign race.

Mr. Huertis rejoined that he could destroy any number of armed men, on the swiftest horses, before they could approach him, as the chief had already seen ; and since he could enforce his exit from the city whenever he thought proper; he would enter it upon his own terms, either as a conqueror, or as a friend, according to the reception he met with. Without waiting for further colloquy, he ordered his party to dismount restore the horses to their owners, and march with the train of mules toward the city, in the usual style of travel. With this order, his Indians complied very reluctantly; but on assuring them that is was a matter of the highest policy, they evinced their wonted confidence in his judgment and ability. To the young chief he returned his richly-caparisoned steed, which had fallen to the lot of the unfortunate Mr. Hammond; who was now lying desperately wounded, in the care of the faithful Antonio. For himself and Senor Velasquez, Mr. Huertis retained the horses they had first seized, and placing themselves on each side of the Iximayan commander, with their friend Hammond borne immediately behind them, in one of the cane couches of the cavern, on the backs of two mules yoked together, they advanced to the head of their party while the red troopers, followed by the surviving bloodhounds leashed in couples, brought up the rear. Huertis, however, had taken the precaution to add the spears and hatchets of these men to the burthens of the forward mules, to abide the event of his reception at the city gates. The appearance of the whole cavalcade was unique and picturesque; for whilst Velasquez wore the uniform of a military company to which he belonged in San Salvador, much enhanced in effect by some brilliant additions, and crowned with a broad sombrero and plume, Huertis wore that of an American naval commander, with gold epaulettes; his riflemen and muleteers generally were clothed in blue cotton and grass hats, while the native cavalry, in the brilliant tunics and feathered coronals, already described, must have completed the diversity of the variegated *cortége* Had poor Hammond been mounted among them, his costume would have been as equivocal as his new complexion for he had attired himself in the scarlet coat of a British officer of rank, with several blazing stars of glass jewels, surmounted by a white Panama hat, in which clustered an airy profusion of ladies' ostrich feathers, dyed blue at the edges.

In passing the spot of the recent skirmish, they found that nine horses and two men had been killed, the latter unintentionally, besides the riflemen their own party. Many other horses were lying wounded, in the struggles of death, and several of their riders were seated on the ground, disabled by bruises or dislocations. Huertis's men buried their comrade in a grave hastily dug with the spears which lay around him, while the Iximayans laid their dead and wounded upon horses, to be conveyed to a village on the plain. The former, it was found, were consumed there the next day, in funeral fires, with idolatrous rites; and it was observed by the travellers that the native soldiers regreted their dead with emotions of extreme sensibility, and almost feminine grief, like men wholly unaccustomed to scenes of violent death. But the strongest emotion evinced by the young chief throughout their intercourse, was when he heard the word "Iximaya," in interpreting for Huertis. He then seemed to be smitten and subdued, by blank despair, as if he felt that the city and its location were already familiarly known to the foreign world.

As already stated, the distance to the city was about six miles. The expedition found the road to it bordered, on either side, as far as the eye could reach, with a profuse vegetation, a portion the result of assiduous and skilful culture.

Indigo, corn, oats, a curious five-eared wheat, gourds, pine-apples, esculent roots, pulse, flax, and hemp, the white as well as the crimson cotton, vineyards, and fruit orchards, grew luxuriantly in large regularly divided fields, which were now ripe for the harvest. The villages, large and populous, were mostly composed of flat-roofed dwellings with broad over-hanging eaves or architraves, supported by heavy columns, often filleted over spiral flutings, in the Egyptian style. A profusion of bold sculpture was the prevailing characteristic, and perhaps defect of all. The inhabitants, who thronged the wayside in great numbers, appeared excited with surprise and exultation, on beholding the large company of strangers appa-rently in the custody of their military; while the disarmed condition of the latter, and the bodies of the slain, were a mystery they could not explain. Many of the husbandmen were observed to be in possession of bows and arrows, and some of the women held rusty spears. The predominant costume of both sexes was a pale blue tunic, gathered in at the breast and decending to the knee, with reticulated buskins, of red cord, covering the calf of the leg. The woman, with few exceptions, were of fine form, and the highest order of Indian beauty, with an extraordinary affluence of black hair, tastefully disposed. At the village where the dead and wounded were left, with their relatives and friends, doleful lamentations were heard, to the time the expedition entered the city.

The walls of this metropolis were forty feet high, slop-ing inward from the foundation, surmounted by a parapet which overhung in a concave curve and rested upon a plain moulding. They were evidently a massive work of a remote period, for although constructed of large blocks of granite stone, white and glittering in the sun, passing ages had cor-roded rough crevices between the layers, and the once perfect cornices had become indented by the tooth of time. The sculptured annals of the city gave them an antiquity of four thousand years. They formed a parallelogram four miles long and three in width, thus inclosing an area of nearly twelve square miles, and breasted the cardinal points of the horizon with a single gate, the midway on every side. On approaching the eastern gate, the travellers discovered that the foundations of the walls were laid in a deep fosse or moat a hundred feet wide, nearly full to its brink, and abounding with water-fowl. It was replenished from the mountains, and discharged its

VALESQUEZ AND COMPANIONS INTRODUCED TO THE EMPEROR.

ALESQUEZ AND COMPANIONS INTRODUCED TO THE EMPEROR.

surplus waters into the lakes of the valley. It was to be crossed by a drawbridge now raised over the gate, and the parapet was thronged with the populace to behold the entrance of so large a number of strangers, for whom there was no return.

At a signal from the young chief, the bridge slowly descended and the cavalcade passed over ; but the folding gates, which, were composed of blocks of stone curiously dovetailed together, and which revolved upon hinges of the same material by a ball and socket contrivance above and below, were not yet opened, and the party were detained on the bridge. A small oval orifice only appeared, less than a human face, and an ear was applied there to receive an expected word in a whisper. This complied with, the ponderous gates unfolded, and a vista of solemn magnificence was presented to the view. It was a vista at once of massive statues and trees, extending, apparently the whole length of the city. No two of the statues were precisely alike in countenance, and very few in their sculptural costume. There was some distinctive emblem upon each. They stood sixty feet apart, with a smaller monuments of some mythological animal between each. A similar but shorter avenue, it appears, crossed the city from north to south, having a proportional number of such monuments through its entire extent ; and these two grand avenues, ran through wide areas of greensward richly grouped with lofty trees.

As the cavalcade advanced to the centre of the city, the population assembled to behold the unprecedented spectacle; but the utmost order prevailed, and the silence was profound. The fact of these strangers wielding deadly weapons had already excited their dread. Arrived at the quadrated point, where the two great avenues intersected, Mr. Huertis boldly demanded of his guide the further course and character of his destination. He was answered by his dignified companion, that he would be conducted to the building immediately before him, one of majestic dimensions and style, where the monarch of the nation daily assembled with his councillors, at the hour of noon, to administer justice and listen to complaints. In the meantime, his wounded friend could be placed in a state of greater ease and repose, in one of the apartments of the edifice, while the mules and baggage could be disposed of in its basement vaults. When this was accomplished; the hour of audience had arrived,

The entire party of strangers, with the young chief and several of his subordinates, were then led into a large and lofty hall, surrounded by columns, and displaying three raised seats covered with canopies of drapery. On the one of these which stood at the eastern end, sat the monarch, a personage of grave but benignant aspect, about sixty years of age, arrayed in scarlet and gold, and having a golden image of the rising sun, of extraordinary splendour, displayed from behind his throne. On the seat on the southern and western side, sat venerable men of advanced age, scarcely less gorgeously attired. Around the apartment, and on the steps of the throne, were other grave-looking men, in scarlet robes, Huertis, Velasquez, and their Indians, still carrying their loaded rifles, of which he had not suffered them to be deprived, stood on the left side of the monarch, the young chief and his soldiers on the right. The latter gave his statement apparently with truth and manly candour, the facts which he averred seeming to fill the whole council with amazement, and to leave settled gloom upon the imperial brow. The decision given, which was concurred in by the associate councillors, and appeared to be that the strangers having magnanimously released and restored the company of guards after they had surrendered themselves prisoners, and having voluntarily entered the city in a peaceable manner, when they might possibly have effected their escape, were entitled to their personal freedom, and might eventually, under certain obligations, become eligible to all the privileges of citizenship, within the limits of the city. Meanwhile they were to make no use of their dangerous weapons, nor exhibit them to terrify the people. With this decision, Huertis and his companions were perfectly satisfied, for the latter had undiminished confidence in his ability and determined to achieve their escape. On leaving the hall of justice, they observed the elder military chief, of whom a slight mention has been made, brought in with two others of inferior rank; and it was afterwards currently reported that they had been sentenced to close imprisonment. It was also ascertained by Velasquez, that the four companies of rangers, already noticed, composing a regiment of two hundred men, constituted the whole military force of this timid peaceful people.

The place of residence assigned to our travellers, was the vacant wing of a spacious and sumptuous structure, at the western extremity of the city, which had been appropriated,

THE PAGAN TEMPLE IN THE CITY OF IXIMAYA

from time immemorial, to the surviving remnant of an ancient and singular order of priesthood called Kaanas, which, it was distinctly asserted in their annals and traditions, had accompanied the first migration of this people from the Assyrian plains. Their peculiar and strongly distinctive lineaments, it is now perfectly well ascertained, are to be traced in many of the sculptured monuments of the central American ruins, and were found still more abundantly on those of Iximaya. Forbidden, by inviolably sacred laws, from intermarrying with any persons but those of their own caste, they had here dwindled down, in the course of many centuries, to a few insignificant individuals, diminutive in stature. They were, nevertheless, held in high veneration and affection by the whole Iximayan community, probably as living specimens of an antique race nearly extinct. Their position as an order of priesthood, it is now known, had not been higher for many ages, if ever, than that of religious mimes and bacchanals, in a certain class of pagan ceremonies, highly popular with the multitude. This, indeed, is evident from their characteristics in the sculptures. Their ancient college, or hospital, otherwise vacant and forlorn, was now chiefly occupied by a much higher order of priests, called Mayaboons, who were their legal and sacerdotal guardians. With a Yachin, one of the junior brethren of this order, named Vaalpeor a young man of superior intellect and attainments, Velasquez soon cultivated a friendly and confidential acquaintance, which proved reciprocal and faithful. And while Huertis was devoting all his time and energies to enquiry respecting this unknown city and people, the ear of this young pagan priest was as eagerly imbibing, from the lips of Velasquez, a similar knowledge of the world at large to him equally new and enchanting. If Huertis had toiled so severely, and hazarded so much, both as to himself and companions, to acquire a knowledge of this one city and people, it soon became clear to the penetrating mind of Velasquez, that Vaalpeor possessed enough both of mental ambition and personal energy, to incur equal toil and risk to learn the wonders of the cities and races of the greater nations of mankind. Indeed, this desire evidently glowed in his breast with a consuming fever; and when Velaquez, after due observation, proposed the liberation of the whole expedition, with Vaalpeor himself as its protected companion, the now consciously imprisoned pagan, horror-stricken at first, re-

garded the proposition complacently, and finally, with a degre
of delight, regardless of consequences. It was, however,
mutually agreed that the design should be kept secret from
Huertis, until ripe for success. A serious obstacle existed in
his plighted guardianship of the Kaana children, whom he
could abandon only with his life; but even this was not deemed
insurmountable.

In the meantime, Huertis, to facilitate his own objects, had
prevailed upon his entire party to conform in dress and habits
with the community in which they lived. The city was surrounded on all sides by a lofty colonnade, sustaining the upper
esplanade of the city walls, and forming a broad covered walk
beneath, in which the population could promenade, sheltered
from sun and shower. In these places of general resort, the
new citizens appeared daily, until they had become familiarly
known to the greater part of the many thousand inhabitants
of the city. Huertis, moreover, had formed domestic and social
connexions; was the welcome guest of families of the highest
rank, who were fascinated with the information he afforded
them of the external world; had made tacit converts to liberty
of many influential persons; had visited each of the four grand
temples which stood in the centre of the several quadranglar
divisions of the city, and externally conformed to their idolatrous worship. He had even been admitted into some of the
most sacred mysteries of these temples, while Velasquez, more
retired, and avowedly more scrupulous, was content to receive
the knowledge thus acquired, in long conversations by the sick
couch of poor Hammond, now rapidly declining to the grave.
Mr. Hammond's dreadful wound had but partially healed in
the course of several months; his constitution was exhausted,
and he was dying of remittent fever and debility. His chief
regret was that he could not assist his friend Huertis in his
researches and drawings, and determine the place of the city by
astronomical observations which his friends were unable to
take. The day before he died, he was visited by some of the
medical priesthood, who, on seeing numerous light spots upon
his skin, where the preparation with which he had stained it
had disappeared, they pronounced him *a leper*, and ordered
that all intercourse with the building should be suspended.
No explanation would convince them to the contrary, and his
death confirmed them in their opinion. Availing himself of
this opportunity, and under the plea that it was important to

WORSHIP OF THE AZTECS BY THE MAYABOONS, &c.

their safety, Vaalpeor removed the two orphan children in his charge to one of the country temples in the plain, and the idle mules of the strangers were employed to carry tents, couches, and other bulky requisites for an unprovided rural residence. It may be added that he included among them much of the baggage of his new friends, with the greater part of their rifles and ammunition. In the meantime Huertis, Velasquez, and about half of their party were closely confined to the part of the edifice assigned for their occupation. Their friend Hammond had been interred without the walls, in a field appropriated to lepers by the civic authorities. Huertis, was now informed of the plan of escape, but was not ready; he had more drawings to make, and many curiosities to collect. The interdicted period of nine days having expired, the young priest, who had free access to the city at all times, again appeared at their abode and urged an early retreat as the return of the orphan children would soon be required. But Huertis was abroad in the city, and could not be consulted. He remained absent all the day and did not return to his apartments at night. It was so all the next day and night and Velasquez was deeply alarmed. On searching his rooms for his papers, drawings and instruments, for secret transmittal into the country, he found them all removed, including those of Mr. Hammond, which were among them. It was then vainly hoped that he had effected his escape with all his treasures, but his Indians knew nothing of the matter.

Shortly after this discovery, Vaalpeor arrived with its explanation. Huertis had made a confidant of his intended flight, whom he idly hoped would accompany it, and she betrayed him. His offence, after his voluntary vows and his initiation in the sacred mysteries, was unpardonable, and his fate could not be doubted. Indeed, the trembling priest at length admitted that he had been sacrificed in due form upon the high altar of the sun, and that he himself had beheld the fatal ceremony. Huertis, however, had implicated none of his associates, and there was yet a chance of escape. To pass the gates was impossible; but the wall might be descended in the night by ropes, and to swim the moat was easy. This was effected by Velasquez and fifteen of his party the same night; the rest either did not make the attempt or failed, and the faithful Antonio was among them. The fugitives had scarcely reached the secluded retreat of Vaalpeor and mounted their mules, before the low yelp of bloodhounds was heard upon their trail, and soon burst into full cry. But the dogs were somewhat confused by the scent of so many footsteps on the spot at which the party mounted, and did not follow the mules until the horsemen led the way. This afforded time for the fugitives, racing their swift mules at full speed, to reach the opening of the valley, when Velasquez wheeled and halted, for the pursuers were close at hand. A conflict ensued, in which many of the horsemen were slain, and the young kaana received an accidental wound of which he retains the scar. It must suffice to say, that the party eventually secured their retreat without loss of life ; and by break of day they were on a mountainous ridge many leagues from Iximayá. In about fourteen days, they reached Ocosingo, after great suffering. Here Velasquez reluctantly parted with most of his faithful Indians, and here also died Vaalpeor, from the unaccustomed toil and deprivations of the journey. Velasquez, with the two Aztec Children, did not reach San Salvador until the middle of February, when they became objects of the highest interest to the most intellectual classes of that city. As the greatest ethnological curiosities in living form that ever appeared among civilised men, he was advised to send them to Europe for exhibition.

Such is the marvellous story detailed by Velasquez. Containing all the elements which can well stimulate curiosity, it also lays claim to a credence which further enquiry must either substantiate or withdraw. The Aztec Children stand independently as the most wonderful members of the human race, whatever their origin and descent ; yet at the same time all testimony professing to throw light on this, is worthy of calm and considerate attention. To view these children is less to enquire whence they came, than to regard them as they are; to watch the progressive dawn of intelligence, and continually stronger developement of individual characteristics. To see them is an event in the life of the beholder, which will never be forgotten. Were they deformities, without proper lineage or name, excresences, or mere freaks of nature, their history would little merit the enquiry or examination now courted. They are here—the descendants of a people who probably passed over to the American continent at a period too remote to be ascertained, members of a race kept preserved in rocky fastnesses, and now discovered on the eve of physical decline and disappearance. The learned world—those interested in philosophical pursuits, and the countless crowd who would find entertaining

THE ESCAPE FROM IXIMAYA.

and rational amusement, have the opportunity of witnessing what will afford material for information, reflection and enjoyment for while a thousand new inventions of a startling character are annually brought before the public mind, and not only their existence admitted, but their practical utility demonstrated, and in an age when, with all its enlightenment, the credulity of mankind stretches even beyond the boundary of the material world, and seeks to make itself the familiar with the unfathomable nature of spiritual existences, a phenomenon in ethnology, combining all the fact of the former with the singularity of the latter, must prove of intense and startling interest.

The discovery of the New World has been followed by a series of revelations in natural history, which have increased the earth's volume of wonders to a vast extent. The geographical features of the two Americas, furnish a panorama of pictures which, for beauty and magnificence, is without parallel.

From where the silver sea of Lake Superior opens its broad mirror of bright waters in a dark northern forest hard by the regions of snow, to where the mighty Mississippi creeps on from a shining thread or skein of water, until, in three thousand miles' journey, it swells the Gulf of Mexico, both continents, on to where the Amazon leaps from the Andes and sweeps through the equatorial valley four thousand miles to the sea, all is full of the most romantic interest.

That description, which elsewhere would be mere grandiloquence and hyperbole, in this region runs no fear of being exagerated into an overdrawn or widely-stretched picture. Within the tropics of this western world, the lands are rich in vestiges of a civilisation which bear a parallel of comparison with the classic grounds of Memphis, Thebes, Baalbec, and Nineveh; and could each monument which now stands a moss-covered sphinx, be read through its hieroglyphics, we should have doubtless a history of empire as varied and remarkable as that which has made Greece and Rome the Mecca of all pilgrims of antiquarian lore. But, alas! no patient inquirer has found a Rosetta Stone as a key to unlock their mysteries, and more sad than all are the ruthless acts by which blind and bigoted fanaticism has annihilated the written record and fractured history of mighty and wonderful nations, the evidence of whose greatness still exists in the marble monuments and wrecks of great cities, which even the iron hand of Time has not been able to obliterate. But the outrage of the Caliph Omar, who fired the Alexandrian library, or the Goths, Vandals and Huns who sacked, pillaged, and over-ran Rome, is palliated by the fact that their barbarity could not destroy *all* the historic lore and treasures of art in the realms which they devastated.

But what shall be said of those who, professing to follow the precepts of our holy Christian religion, madly fall to work to exterminate not only the race of men who filled this western world, but for ever sealed in oblivion the unoffending archives of their history? How must every scholar and liberal mind detest the deplorable madness which urged the insane zealot *Zumarraga* to gather the thousand glorious volumes and endless scrolls of illuminated maps which contained every portion of Aztec history, and make of them one huge funeral pyre, in the great square of Mexico, by the Temple of Mexitli, as an offering to the blind spirit of superstition.

What shall we say of the destruction of the MSS in 830, pages gathered by that glorious liberal-hearted, Christian priest, Bartolomé Las Casas (first bishop of Chiapas), which Ramesal put in the library of the Dominicans at Valladolid; and also "A General History of America," in three volumes, folio, in the library of the Count Villambrosa, in Madrid, where Sinelo saw it, as he affirms in his " Bibliotheca Occidentali," together with two volumes which he saw in the celebrated archives of Simaneas, which have been the sepulchre of so many precious manuscripts on America.

Or what can ever compensate for the injustice done to that elegant scholar Lorenzo Loturini Bennæducci, of Milan, whose eight years of industry and diligent research gave him numerous select and invaluable MSS of the Aztecs; and whose museum of curiosities was only equalled by that of the learned Carlos de Siguenza E. Gongora, and who, like him, through the excessive jealousy of the Spanish government, was stripped of all his literary estate, and sent to Spain, upon some pseudo religious charge, of which he was acquitted; but sad to say, the force of fanaticism had swallowed up all his labours in his absence, and his mass of MSS were gone for ever. Such a gap made in these national records, caused the sceptical Abbé Raynal to say, afterwards: " Nothing are we permitted to affirm, except that the Mexican empire was governed by Montezuma, at the time that the Spaniards landed on the Mexican coast"—to which the celebrated native Mexican priest, Abbè d' Francesco Saverio Clavigero well replies : " Why not doubt the existance of Montezuma !" If we are permitted to affirm this as ascertained by the testimony of the Spaniards who saw that king, we feel the attestation of the same Spaniards to a vast many other things belonging to the ancient history of Mexico, which were seen by them and confirmed by the depositions of the Indians themselves. Such particulars, therefore, may be affirmed as positively as the existance of Montezuma, or ought, we also to entertain a doubt of *that* ? If there is reason however, to doubt all the ancient history of Mexico, the antiquity of most other nations would come in question, for it is not easy to find another nation, the events of which have been confirmed, by a greater number of historians than those of the Mexicans, nor do we know that any people ever published so severe a law against false historians as that of the Acolhuas.

While in the silence of history it becomes impossible to positively know certain facts, there is little merit, on the other hand, in raising mere doubts by scepticism. For example, we have seen the mere whim urged, that there was no such person as Julius Cæsar or William Shakspere. But the person desirous of investigating and ascertaining the truth in such matters must pass these silly equivocations with contempt. Are we to discredit the existance of a race in the full tide of their prosperity as lately as the year 1521, and account them merely traditionary or chimerical because the roots of giant trees are growing upon the tops of their palaces, and their gorgeous temples buried in the leafy shadows of almost impenetrable forests ? Not at all. Copan, Palenque, Uxmal and Tula, are as well, if not better defined and authenticated than Gizeh's immortal Pyramid of Cheops, or the subterranean labyrinths of the Catacombs. The explorations of Champollion, Layard, and Bayard Taylor upon the borders of the Nile, and among the mighty wrecks which strew the sites of ancient Babylon and Nineveh, are not more strangely interesting than the marvellous cities and giant works of architecture so recently visited by John L. Stephens, Brantz Meyer, Mr. Norman, and Mr. Squieres; and so beautifully illustrated in the great work of Lord Kingsborough, and described with such romantic interest by Prescott, the American historian.

. Without entering into any hypothesis or speculation tuch

ing the identity of Central American monuments and their hieroglyphics, with those of Egypt or the oriental world, or adopting the conjecture of Dr. Siguenza, that St. Thomas, the Apostle was identical with the famous Aztec divinity, Quetzalcoatl (about whose head the sun breathed a perpetual halo, and wherever he travelled preaching the true gospel, corn grew to twice its usual size, fruits were in their fullest perfection, and birds hymned unending harmonies in a blooming paradise), there is, in this wonderful region of Central America, unsurpassed for its natural beauty and delicious climate, a mysterious charm upon every hand, from the multiplicity of ruins scattered around in all directions. Upon the borders of the magnificent Lake Nicaragua, whose banks are covered with palms, which look like so many giant plumes, while the shores are covered with a dense mass of verdure, coming down like a wall to the very edge of the water, there are the broad leaves of the plantain, the gigantic ceiba, the slender cocoa palm, beside a hundred other strange varieties, bound together by vines covered with flowers, and hanging their long pliant tendrils from every stem. In this mass of impenetrable verdure, which never fades, wild screaming parrots and noisy macaws glide in and out ; and there is heard the perpetual chatter of apes and nimble monkeys, leaping from bough to bough, and plucking the golden fruits which cluster upon those tropical trees. And a short distance to the south of this can be found the rival of the fabulous bird Roc of the Arabian Nights, in that giant eagle, the Condor of the Andes. And throughout this portion of Guatemala and Mexico is to be seen almost everywhere the phœnix of the vegetable world, the superb AGAVE AMERICANA, the century plant, which, after receiving the suns of a hundred summers upon its head, blooms but once, and perishes.

But on the other hand we are not to accept everything, touching ancient or modern Mexico, with gross gullibility, such as the History of Mexico by the famous Theodore Bry, or Gage's work, in the general history of the Travels of Prevost, or the great work entitled Ca Galerie Agreable du Mond, which says that "ambassadors were sent in former times to the court of Mexico mounted upon elephants !"

The plain facts are these :—here was a mighty wilderness in the western world rich in its tropical luxuriance, a more than Arcadian region, under the name of Anahuac, the earliest twilight of whose history represents it as the home of a shadowy race called the Olmecs, whom the eye of tradition alone can discover through the thickening obscurity of the past; these were followed by the Toltecs, who were without doubt the Greeks of America, or more nearly resembled in their mighty movements the Phœnician ancestry of the Athenians; the pyramid of Cholula being in all probability coeval with that of Cheops.

"The empire of the Aztecs," (says an American author ?) (by whom the three states of Mexico, Tezuco, and Tlacopan, under the general name of Anahuac, were holden), lasted about two hundred years, when it was conquered by the Spaniards under Cortez, being the same territory which had been possessd by the Toltecs, a race that passed mysteriously away, leaving a multitude of monuments which marked them as a mighty and wonderful people, who never, according to historians, stained their altars with human blood, nor debased their banquets by the still more horrible custom of cannabalism as was the case with their Aztec successors, and also to a certain, but much smaller extent, with the Tezcucans

These Toltecs, who disappeared so mysteriously and unaccountably, were in all probability the founders of those vast cities whose solid superstructures of stone and giant works of architecture rival in beauty and magnificence, even in their ruins, the mighty wrecks which lie scattered in the desert sands of Egypt; but whence these Toltecs came, or whither they have vanished, must remain for ever an inscrutable secret: all that we know is that a wonderful race, far advanced in civilization, once held their home in the Great Valley of Mexico; but when we seek to know their habits or their history, an unseen hand is stretched forth, and an impenetrable curtain of clouds is drawn across the sun of their glory, and we are left standing in double darkness, without a star to light the pathway of our wanderings."

In 1325, the Aztecs descended into the Vale of Mexico, whose Eden-like beauty drew from the honest old soldier of Castile, Bernal Diaz, the exclamation: "When I beheld the scenes which were around me, I thought within myself, 'this was the garden of the world," Fenced in by a circular wall of mountains lay the matchless valley, and shining along it for seventy miles, were the seven silver lakes, including the fresh tide of Chalco, the Sweet Water, and the miniature salt sea of Tezcuco. Within the latter lake, upon the islands of Accocolco, whose bog-like character required them to bring stone from the mainland, they planted the first rude huts, and amid the reeds laid the foundation of an empire, which, in an existance of three hundred years, rose to the pitch of occidental grandeur with a rapidity unparalleled; and from this mimic sea, the Venice of the West lifted her thousand temples and palaces out of the blue bosom of the waters.

By the beginning of the sixteenth century, their sway extended from the Atlantic to the Pacific, from the region of the barbarous Olmecs upon the north, to the farthest limits of Guatemala upon the south. Their language was spoken by seven tribes in and around the Great Valley. They vere the Zochimilcas, Topanecas, Colhuas, Tlahuicas, Mexicans, and Tlascalans. The latter tribe threw off their allegiance, and repulsed by repeated defeat, the other six tribes, had established themselves as an independent republic, some seventy miles from the city of Tenochtitlan, or Mexico, where they remained the rivals for years, and ultimately became the cause of the final overthrow and downfall of the Aztec power.

Of the conquest by Hernando Cortez, it is unnecessary to speak at length, or to tell how he cut his cables, and stood out by night from Cuba in search of the unknown empire of the west, to the time when he planted his triumphant banner of the Cross and of Castile on the pinnacle of the Temple of Mexitli, and was master of the mightiest monarch that ever swayed the rod of empire in the land of the setting sun. Tracing a course with a handful of chivalrous associates, until by unequalled prowess, he had conquered countless hosts, and leagued them to himself and to his cause: how they had started forth a few poor soldiers of fortune-adventurers, whose chief means consisted of a suit of mail or a stout-limbed steed, with scarce ducats enough to have bought a peasent's hut upon the slopes of the Sierra Morena, or a fishermen's shed on the silver shores of the Guadalquiver; by a sudden freak of fortune, and their own indefatigable fortitude and enterprise, suddenly changed to the possessors of riches which would have purchased the palaces of a Venetian duke, or the Doge himself. Thus bidding defiance to Velasquez, in Cuba, and the threatened thunders of the Bishop of Burgos, in Spain, Cortez burst in upon a silent land with his few cavaliers, emerged suddenly on the golden glories of El Dorado and found himself like Sindbad of the Oriental romance, in the midst of the Valley of diamonds.

It is unnecessary to dwell upon this theme, the history of

the conquest of Mexico has grown familiar, and the exploits of chivalry in the New World, have become as classic as the Crusades. The heroism of the last great chieftian of the Aztecs, who bore the barbarian torture of the Christians with unfaltering fortitude, calling the glowing embers, "flowers of fire," draws from the most distinguished of living men, Alexander von Humboldt, the expression—"Ce trait est digne de plus beau temps de la Gréce et de Rome. Sous toutes les zones quelle que soit la couleur des hommes, la langage des âmes fortes lorsqu' elles luttent contre malheur. Nous avons vu plus haut quelle fut la fin tragique de cet infortunê Quauhtemotzin."

Without further pursuing the subject of Aztec history, we will pass on without stopping to speculate too curiously upon the various hypotheses touching the origin of the inhabitants of this portion of America : we will not insist upon their being one of the lost tribes of Israel, as Dr. Siguenza and Lord Kingsborough will have it, nor with certain others, that they are of Siberian origin ; for in their likeness to Jewish or Aztec tribes, there is not sufficient identity, nor even with the Egyptian, warrant an assertion that they are the same race. Of their variance from the North-American Indian (the red men), there needs no proof, even to the most casual observer ; the difference is so distinctive, indeed, from the Caucasian, the Mongolian, the African, and Red American races, that the mere glance is sufficient to carry conviction of their separate individuality as a race ; and the more careful examination of the ethnologist goes but to strengthen the fact of their perfectly distinct character, physiologically and phrenologically.

It might be considered just, with great propriety, to class these remarkable specimens of humanity with fabulous existences, if the truth of their being rested upon mere individual assertion—BUT HERE THEY ARE ! LIVING ! and open to public view and examination—not merely imaginary creatures, like the strange men of Africa mentioned by Herodotus,, the phœnix or the mermaid. Not a fictitious people, like the fauns and dryads of the Arcadian vales—not the moonlight fairies ; the little grey men of the Norse legends—not nymph, sprite, nor elf—but human beings, of flesh and blood—the remnant of a strange and wonderful race—the greatest marvel of the land of wonders, and of the nineteenth century—more strange than the vast skeletons of the Mastodon, which have been exhumed in the same region—but, like the black swan of New Holland formerly regarded as a myth, but now a well-establised existence. In short, as curious and as well substantiated as the singular sightless fish of the mammoth cave in Kentucky.

In brief, these Aztec Children present the most extraordinary phenomenon in the human race ever witnessed by the modern world : let their origin be what it may—let their history and their country's history be ever so vague and traditionary —doubt the truth of Velasquez's narrative or believe it wholly—these children present in themselves the eighth wonder of the world. They are, without exception, the most remarkable and intensely interesting objects that were ever presented to the European public.

In America they have been the marvel of a million beholders, and wherever they travel they must become the centre of attraction of every inquiring mind, and will doubtless prove a puzzle to the profoundest philosophers and ethnologists of the age.

All the learned and scientific men in the United States have submitted them to critical examination, and unite in pronouncing them the most unique and extraordinary beings that have ever fallen under observation.

The attention of European men of science, ethnologists phyiologists, philosophers, and physicians, is now called to these most curious and remarkable children. They are requested to examine and fully investigate what the scientific men of America have united in pronouncing the most startling and extraordinary curiosity that has been exhibited in the present century.

MEASUREMENTS OF THE AZTECS.

Taken by Professor Owen the 30th day of June, 1853, in London prior to the convening of a special Meeting, of the Ethnological society the President Sir Benjamin Brodie, and Secretary R. Cull, Esq: which was attended by all its members and by many Medical celebritie·

	BOY.(*Maximo*) 17 years of age.		GIRL. (*Bartola*) 11 years.	
	inches	lines	inches	lines
Height from sole to vertex	34	6	30	9
Length of Spinal Column	16	0	15	8
Arm (Humerus)	7	0	6	6
Ulna	5	9	5	3
Hand	4	0	4	2
Breadth of Hand	2	3	2	0
Length of Thumb	1	0	1	3
Middle Finger	2	0	2	0
Little Finger	0	11	1	3
Femur	9	3	8	6
Tibia	8	7	7	0
Foot	5	0	4	7
Circumference of Chest, under axillœ	?0	5	19	7
Pelvis	17	6	17	0

The great Toe is well developed and the Foot otherwise well formed in both.

	Weight 23lbs		21½lbs.	
Circumference of Cranium (Head)	13	3	13	4
Antero-posterior diameter	4	3	4	6
Transverse diameter	3	9	3	10
From one Meatus Auditorius to the other				
around the Forehead	7	6	7	2
Ditto over the Vertex	7	9	8	2
Ditto around the Occiput	5	7	5	5
From root of nose over Head to the				
occipital-spine	7	10	8	2
Length of nose	2	9		

MEASUREMENTS *in Dec.* 1850, *by Dr. Warren,*(*Boston, America.*
"Dr. Warren, has been very minute in his examination.'

"Boy.—Height	33¾ inches.
Spine	16
Arm (humerus)	6¾
Forearm	5½

Hand, length	Breadth 2
Femur	
Tibia	
Left lower extremity	Foot 5 inch.
Circumference of chest	
" waist	
" pelvis	

HEAD.—Circumference over hair
    Antero-posterior diameter
    Bi-temporal diam. not quite
    From one auditory passage
      to other, around forehead
    Do. over top of head -
    Do. around the occiput
    Fronto-occipital curve
    Ear
    Facial angle -

The pulse, observed at different times, varied from 80 to 100 irregular in rhythm, much increased on the slightest exertion.

GIRL.—Pulse regular, from 80 to 90. Resp. 20.

Height	$29\frac{1}{2}$ inches.	
Spine	$15\frac{1}{2}$	
Humerus	6	
Ulna	5	
Hand	4	
Lower extremity	15	Foot $4\frac{1}{2}$ inches.
Circumference of chest	19	
" waist	16	
" pelvis	16	
Head	13 in circumference.	
Antero-posterior diameter	$4\frac{3}{4}$	
Lateral "	$3\frac{3}{4}$	
Over top of head, from one au-		
ditory passage to the other	8	
Ear - - -	$1\frac{3}{4}$	

The head of an infant at birth was as follows
    Ant.-post, diameter
    Bi-temporal   "
    Circumference
    Over top of head from ear to ear
    Occipito-frontal -

CPSIA information can be obtained
at www.ICGtesting.com
Printed in the USA
BVOW06s1210270217
477251BV00015B/214/P